MAKING MONEY EASILY IN NIGERIA

FIRST WAY TO MAKE MONEY EASILY

CHRISTOPHER ABRAHAM

DEDICATION

This book is dedicated to my friends and students who are yet to lay hands on this content

CONTENTS

1 Introduction

2 10 Bitter Truths No One Ever Told You about Online Business

3 How to Choose the Right Online Business for You

4

Choosing the Right Niche

5

How to Create a Blog Using Blogger (A Step-by-step Guide)

6 A Beginners' Guide to SEO (Search Engine Optimization)

7 8 Foolproof Tips for Attracting Traffic to Your Blog Posts

8 Ethical Link Building: All You Need to Know

9 How to Quickly Increase Your Blog's Profit Potential

10 5 Ways You Can Receive Payment Online (Aside PayPal)

CHAPTER ONE

INTRODUCTION

Firstly, I want to thank you for downloading this e-book. I greatly appreciate it.

So you want to establish an online business that will boost your income or even replace your offline income streams? In this e-book, you'll learn exactly how to do that.

If you diligently implement all the tips you're about to learn, you'll end up setting up a powerful blog that will make you hundreds of dollars per month through various online income streams – active and passive. (Note the words "active" and "passive." I'll explain what they mean in the first lesson.)

Now, let's get started...

What exactly is my goal with this e-book?

Before we go any further, it's important that I remind you of what I want to help you achieve – ***I want to help you set up a blog that has the potential to generate $100 or more per week.***

You may think that's too small. But keep in mind that we have to start from somewhere, and that the stated amount ($100/week) is not our upper limit. It may just be the stepping-stone on your journey to earning much more. If you can gather the necessary skills and confidence to achieve this "little" goal, then you can easily multiply the success either by expanding your blog or by creating more blogs.

So, for now, let's stay put with our "little" goal of $100 per week. Agreed? Great!

I advise you to implement EVERY tip I share with you. That's the only way you can prove to me that I'm not like an excited motivational speaker mounting the podium in an empty hall.

I want to assume that you have no previous experience in online business. So, there may be times I'll have to take my time to explain some concepts (that you may already have known) in full detail.

Also, I may purposely leave a concept unexplained because I intend to cover it in full detail later on. For example, the topic of monetizing your blog comes up around the end of the e-book. So, please bear with me at all times.

If you don't fully understand a concept, read again to see if I promised to explain it later. If I didn't, you've probably missed out something. In that case, don't hesitate to contact me for an explanation.

Also, I want to make this clear: I believe strongly in going about anything the legitimate way. There are tons of shortcuts and illegitimate ways to make money online, but you can never have peace of mind by trailing those paths. Besides, your success would be short-lived. So, I'll never teach you how to set up, promote, or monetize your online business in ways that are unethical.

In this e-book, I'll be teaching you how to set up your own online business in a brick-by-brick fashion. So, never skip any of my tips and recommendations. (I'm sure you don't like to build an incomplete house.)

Now, let me speak directly to your mind...

I know you're really itching to set up your blog, market it, and start making money.

But calm down, my friend. A long journey starts with a single step. So, let's be gradual in our approach.

Now, I won't hide any truths. Online business is not as rosy as some people may have made you to believe. But I can offer tips that will help ease your journey towards setting up a successful online business.

There WILL be times when this business is very hard, when nothing seems to be going your way, and when you feel like quitting. These are natural states that we all experience. The golden secret is to remain determined and not give in to them. You must learn how to handle these situations and feelings.

There's this one thing I can guarantee with absolute clarity: If you don't take the steps I'll share in this course, you won't achieve the expected results.

So, prepare your mind for success by having a strong resolve to implement everything you learn. If you do, in the near future, you'll look back with pride at what you've accomplished.

On a final note, build a habit of success...

Most of the things we do in life are simply habits that have been formed through repetition. We can use this to our advantage, but most of the time we do not. Many of our habits are negative and destructive. We have habits of negative thoughts, wasting time, overeating, overspending, etc.

Your success with this e-book will depend on whether or not you take the actions that I prescribe. Why not take advantage of the incredible power of habits and use it for your own good?

Keep in mind that I've presented all the lessons from my own perspective. It won't hurt if, after reading a lesson, you research the web for more information about the content of the lesson. (And if you come across some information that leaves you confused, send me an email.)

To succeed in online business, more of your spare time should go into learning and implementing – consistently. Not "Facebooking" or "Twittering" for hours. Not reading celebrity gist that adds no good to your life.

So, read this e-book, implement whatever you learn, ask questions when necessary, be determined to succeed, and you'd be very fine in the end.

Getting Started: An Introduction to Online Business Though there are many definitions for online business, here's the one that I deem most apt for our discussion here:

Online business is one that is operated via the internet and that brings income via the internet as well (my definition).

In online business, your website or blog is your showroom/store where you display your wares and skills and convince prospects that you offer quality.

There are two types of online business: active and passive

An active online business is one that requires you to render specific services or requires your active participation in some other way. Most of the time, the profit you'll make from an active business is proportionate with your activity.

For instance, I'm a freelance writer. So, my monthly income is based on how many writing assignments I complete within a month. If I decide not to write, then I won't make money.

Your online business would be an active one if you render services such as ghost-writing, graphics design, SEO, programming, virtual assistance, data entry, etc.

A passive online business is one that brings income continuously even when you're not actively involved.

But does that mean you're not required to do anything? No.

In fact, for you to make money through passive means, you must have invested lots of time, effort, and even money right from the beginning. Only after you've built your business perfectly can you sit back and enjoy the fruits of your labour. So, passive online businesses also require hard work (even more than active businesses).

When a passive business starts to generate profits, there's no limit to the income you can make from it. And you can continue to make money even when you're sleeping (that why it's called "passive").

Examples of passive online businesses include affiliate marketing and information marketing (you'll know more about these later).

The bottom line is that both active and passive online businesses require hard work.

So, if a self-proclaimed "genius" somewhere is promising to teach you how to make thousands of dollars overnight or at the click of a button, quickly raise your bullshit detectors and look elsewhere.

PS. Sports betting, investing in HYIP schemes, and being paid to read emails or completing surveys are ways by which people make money online. But they're not real online businesses. A real business is what you own, run, and have control over the income it brings. So, I only teach real businesses that have permanent profit potentials.

With the above in mind, let's look at the tools you'll need to start an online business.

No, you don't need to be a programmer or a graduate in marketing or writing. And you don't need a huge amount of cash to get started, either. Here is a short list of all that you need:

- A computer (laptop, desktop, etc.)
- A reliable internet connection
- Basic computer skills (browsing the internet, typing, performing simple computer operations such as uploading images, etc.)
- Minimal writing skills. I stress the word "minimal." All you need is a basic ability to express yourself clearly.
- $10 per year to register your domain name. Plus, hosting fees (this varies depending on your chosen host) if you're not going for a free hosting platform.
- Most importantly, a strong determination to learn

and take action, and the zeal to succeed.
Having understood all that has been stated, it's very important that you know the hard sides of online business, as this will help prepare your mind for the challenges ahead. You'll learn these in the next lesson.

CHAPTER TWO
10 BITTER TRUTHS NO ONE EVER TOLD YOU ABOUT ONLINE BUSINESS

"Here's how I'm making 4-figures monthly from my blog. I've quit my day job, and I'm now my own boss."

"How I made thousands of dollars within one month selling information products."

"Revealed: How I'm making at least $500 daily from Fiverr."

"Here are my secrets: How I'm making $10,000 monthly through affiliate marketing."

"How I make my living from website and domain flipping."

I'm sure you've run into more than enough enticing headlines like these. And I'm sure that each time you read such success stories, the zeal rekindles in you to kick-start your own online business.

Yes, you've learned – from hundreds of stories – that the internet is a goldmine, and that you can lead the lifestyle of your dreams by venturing into online business. My friend, that's very true. But there's more to online business...

There are many bitter truths about online business that most successful people leave out in their success stories (for reasons I just don't understand). And I'll be revealing some of them here.

After reading this post, you'll be making either of these two statements to yourself:

- "Oh I never knew it's like this. Nobody told me all these before. I thought it was rosier. I'm no longer interested."

- "No problem. I know success doesn't come easy. I'm ready to face the challenge."

The first thought will prompt you to quit early, thereby saving you from getting frustrated and embittered by the harsh realities. The second will keep you going – even when things seem to have turned sour – and spur you on to the point of success. So, both thoughts have advantages.

Here are 10 of the bitter truths most online money-spinners never told you about online business:

1. Without traffic, your online business is dead

The major task before every online entrepreneur is to attract traffic. Only when you achieve this can you make decent profit from your online business. Your blog's useless if you only get unit count visits daily – by your siblings and friends.

To make real money – not crumbs – from online business, you need huge traffic. Think thousands to millions. The more traffic you generate; the more income you'll make.

No business would thrive without customers, and online business isn't an exception. Generating traffic is like attracting customers.

2. You'll need determination and hard work

As of present, there are several millions of websites and blogs on the internet. And over 100,000 new blogs are created daily by people like you – those who want to make money online.

Those statistics imply that online business is a competition – one that only the dogged and undaunted can win. No matter what aspect of online business you're eyeing, the truth is, several thousands of people are already into it.
So, it's a survival-of-the-fittest thing. Only those who are ready to face the Darwinian test will succeed in online business.

3. Online business is not rosy, especially from the start

Have you been thinking that all you need to do is create your web page, publish some articles you scraped from other sites, litter your sidebar with ads and affiliate links, and sit back to watch your income soar? My friend, you've been dreaming! So wake up now. Online business isn't that rosy. You'll need to set up a web page or blog that looks very professional and attractive. You'll need to write and publish several articles.

Now, not just articles – unique, valuable, and error-free articles that will engage your audience and position you as an expert in your chosen niche.

You'll need to spend time on monitoring your analytics and traffic, keyword research, finding new post ideas, experimenting with SEO techniques, and so on.

In short, you'll need to spend lots of time, energy, and money. That's the fact!

4. Google is king

Any online business not indexed by Google is NOT online. That's the truth, my friend.
Google is the most popular search engine. It is the most consistent source of traffic for high-ranking sites. And that's why the battle for the top spots in Google's rankings will

forever remain a very fierce one.

The dream of online entrepreneurs is to see their websites in the top spots in Google's rankings. And they're all striving hard to realize this dream. If you're serious about your online business, this should be your dream, too.

To get your desired online visibility, you must always play by Google's rules. Any attempt to play games with almighty Google will leave you badly burned in the end.

4. Specificity is the shortcut to online business success

If you're thinking of starting a blog on general health and wellness, I'll advise you to drop that idea. Do you know why? Because that niche is very huge and already dominated by some monster sites (like WebMD, Mayo Clinic, Medline, etc.) that you can never topple in the rankings for most keywords, no matter how hard you try.

Instead, streamline your focus by blogging on a smaller niche like health tips for pregnant women, weight loss tips for busy and lazy people, etc. This way, you'll quickly achieve success due to the specificity of the niche.

So, it's either you narrow your focus, or you fizzle out!

5. You can't make money overnight

You've come across adverts like, *"start making thousands of dollars within 24 hours"*, or *"fill up your bank account at the click of a button."* Yes, I'm sure you've come across them. But do you need someone to tell you that they're nothing but blatant lies and scams?

See, you can't make money overnight from online business. Darren Rowse (ProBlogger), John Chow, Seth Godin, Neil Patel, and others who are earning 4-5 figures monthly from their online businesses never succeeded overnight. It took some of them years of dedication and hard work before they struck gold.

Now, I'm not saying you can't start making money within a shorter timeframe. In fact, you can start making money 6 months after starting your online business, or even sooner, depending on the type of business. But bear in mind that you won't start making money immediately.

Dump the idea of making money right from the start. Rather, focus on building a large audience, building trust, and positioning yourself as an expert in your chosen niche. Once you've achieved all these, you'll easily convince people to take whatever action you want from them. And that's when your profit will start flowing in ceaselessly.

But you can't achieve all these overnight. No, you can't.

6. You must be ready to write frequently or pay someone to do that

Google ranks websites based on content and back-links. The more articles you write (around your target keywords) and publish, and the more frequently you publish new articles, the higher Google ranks your blog. That's one thing you should keep in mind.

Another thing is that, in order to attract and convince your audience to stay glued to your blog, you must publish high quality, unique articles that readers will find valuable.

Truth is, for each topic that you can think of writing about, thousands of articles have already been published about that same topic. So, to really wow your readers, you must present your content from a fresh perspective that will engage them. If you publish crappy articles, you'll only raise their bullshit detectors and repel them.

So, to succeed in online business, you must be ready to write high quality content. Better yet, hire a professional writer (like me) to do the job for you.

7. Shortcuts are dangerous

Many people think they can adopt various dubious techniques and get away with them. Remember, on the web, Google is not lax; it's a strict cop. So, if you play any funny games, you'll get busted!

Avoid publishing content stolen from other websites. If you do, Google will penalize your website or blog for duplicate content. Of course, Google has a way of finding out the original owner of a post (perhaps, by the date of publication). And websites featuring stolen content are either demoted or delisted from the rankings.

Also, avoid building spam back-links. There are many programs online promising to create thousands of back-links to your website or blog within hours. Avoid these like a plague. If you use them, you'll get burned in the end.

In short, avoid any tactic that seems to be a shortcut. Of course, you may get good results from such, but your joy would be short-lived, I'm telling you.

8. SEO and traffic tips "live" and "die"

This is another bitter truth. As of present, I still see many webmasters wasting their precious time on search engine optimization and traffic generation tactics that have long lost their effectiveness.

Fact is, most SEO techniques that worked magically a few

years back are no longer effective. Similarly, the effective techniques of the present may lose all their significance in the coming months or years.

So, you must keep abreast with the latest trends in SEO and traffic generation. No tactic is guaranteed to retain its effectiveness permanently – except publishing quality content.

9. Tactics that worked magically for others may not work for you

That's just it! If I should reveal how I've been making a living from freelance writing for the past two years, and you were to adopt all my tactics perfectly, you still may end up not making any money. So, no tactic guarantees success in online business. (I think that's where some traces of luck come in.)

Similarly, if Darren Rowse were to explain in full detail how he built a blog that now earns him 5-figures monthly, and you were to replicate his steps, you may end up making much less – even though you did everything he did. But it's a two-sided thing. You may also end up making more than he did. That's possible, too.

Does that mean you shouldn't learn from the experts? No. Follow their steps, but keep in mind the fact that there's no guarantee you'll succeed with the same tactics as much as they did.

So, don't cry foul after you've paid for a coaching course and the tactics you learned don't seem to work. It happens.

10. Online business involves lots of trial-and-error

Yes, you'll need to carry out many experiments if you want to succeed in online business. Sometimes, you may have to risk losing money, just to find out what will bring results and what will not.

As I stated earlier, not all proven techniques will work for you. So, you need to keep trying different ones to know which works. If you're the type that hates experimenting, I'm sorry, online business isn't for you.

Bottom line...

You'd agree with me that these truths aren't encouraging. But I have to reveal them because nobody else is doing the same.

I'm sure one of the two thoughts I listed earlier is lingering in your mind right now. I mean, right now you're either thinking of dumping your online business idea or considering taking the bull by the horns.

If you're really in for online business, then don't let anything stop you. Read on…

CHAPTER THREE
HOW TO CHOOSE THE RIGHT ONLINE BUSINESS FOR YOU?

There are several ways to make money online, but many of them are not "real businesses."

Truly, people are making cool money from sports betting and "get paid-to" schemes (where they're paid to real emails or complete surveys). But the truth is, they are not real businesses, and serious minded people shouldn't waste their time on these risky or timewasting ventures.

A real online business is one that you own, control, and bear full responsibility for its successes and failures *(my definition)*.

If you really want to make money online over a long period, then set up a real business.

The following are real online businesses that are very lucrative:

1. Information marketing

2. Affiliate marketing

3. Freelancing

4. Website flipping

5. Blogging

(I have explained these businesses briefly in the previous lesson.) Now, how do you make the right choice from among these businesses?

Of course, you can easily combine two or more of these businesses. But you have to start with one, which should be based on your passion, knowledge, or skills.

Let me start with businesses that are for specific categories of people.

Freelancing is for you if you have skills such as writing, website design and development, programming, data entry, search engine optimization, graphics design, video creation, editing, translation, video transcription, and so on.

Website flipping is for you if you're a prolific writer, and you are patient enough to develop a website from scratch into a money spinner. Better yet, you must be ready to spend lots of cash on content creation if you're not a good writer yourself.

To start a website flipping business, you must have moderate to advanced knowledge of SEO, website transfer between hosts, HTML and CSS, and so on. So, this business may not be very suitable for beginners.

Information marketing is for you if you have some knowledge or skill that many people are yearning to learn. Or if you're very good at researching the web and collating high quality information that will solve people's problems, end their worries, and answer their questions.

In addition, to succeed as an information marketer, you must be very good at marketing and writing compelling sales copies that will convince and convert prospects quickly.

Now, let's look at online businesses that anyone can start and succeed at:

Blogging and **affiliate marketing** are two online

businesses that anyone can venture into.

As an affiliate marketer, you can market any product that is related to your chosen business. And you can make a lot of money from that.

Blogging is the mother of all online businesses. Even if you're going into freelancing, affiliate marketing, or information marketing, having a blog around your business will boost your profit in the long run.

In addition, if you have no services to render as a freelancer or no information product to market, blogging would still be suitable for you. Just start a blog around a topic that interests you, develop it and you'll make money through various means – Adsense, affiliate marketing, private ads, sponsored review posts, etc.

So, which option best for you?

Well, it depends on your knowledge, skills, passion, and interest. Think about these and figure out the right business for you. You can start with a list of options and then narrow down to the best.

Key Terms in Online Business That You Must Understand

Here is a glossary of terms that are frequently used in online business. (Pardon me, but I'll assume that you're a complete beginner who has no idea what any of these terms mean.)

1. Search engine

This is a program designed to help retrieve information from the internet. Google is the most commonly used search engine. Other popular search engines of great importance to internet entrepreneurs are Yahoo and Bing.

SERPs (search engine result pages) are the pages on which search results are displayed after a query.

2. Keyword

A keyword is a word or phrase that is used by online entrepreneurs in search engine optimization. Keywords are gathered based on how people enter their queries while searching for information on the web.

For example, assume you're an affiliate marketer who sells products that cure acne.

If you discover, during a keyword research, that many people who want to buy treatments for acne are searching Google using the query *"acne cure"*, you will simply pick this query as your keyword and optimize your website/blog for it. This will make your website show up in Google's results pages when people search Google with the query.

3. Keyword research

This is the process of finding out the queries that people use to search the web for relevant information.

Keyword research helps you know which keywords to optimize your website/blog for. It also gives you hints on the type of information that your target audience are looking for.

4. Long tail keyword

A long tail keyword (or a long tail) is simply a keyword phrase that comprises four words and more. Though they attract less traffic, long tails are very important because they are more specific, and they attract specific visitors that are likely to fetch you money.

For example, if you're an affiliate marketer for acne cure products, your blog would offer relevant information such as the definition, causes, and home remedies of acne – with your affiliate links subtly sprinkled within your content.

Even though you discuss the causes of acne on your blog, your aim is to attract visitors who would buy the product through your affiliate links, not those who would visit your blog just to learn the causes of acne and hit the close button.

In order to streamline your targeted visitors to only those who would buy the products you're marketing, you'd have to target a keyword phrase like *"buy acne cure online"* or any other related keyword discovered to be commonly used by consumers.

Now get this: If you target a more generic keyword, such as *"acne cure"*, you'll attract more visitors. But your visitors in this case would include those who want to learn how to cure acne with diet, home remedies for acne, herbs for curing acne, etc. Of course, these people are of no use to you. You only need those who are ready to buy a product from an online store. If you target only such visitors, you'll make more money because they'll click on your affiliate links and buy the products you're marketing (even though you'll generate less traffic).

5. Content

Content is a collective term referring to the information – in any format – that you offer on your website or blog. It could be text, images, video, mp3, slideshow, etc.

Text remains the best format in which content is offered. This is because search engines analyze only the text on a page to figure out what the page is all about. Also, text is easily accessible for all users (some browsers may not display images properly and some visitors may not want to download mp3 and video files due to their usually large size).

Quality content refers to information that readers or visitors find very valuable because it answers their questions, solves their problems, or teaches them something new. You must offer this type of content all the time, to attract repeat visitors.

6. Search engine optimization

Search engine optimization (SEO) is the practice that involves implementing certain tactics aimed at improving the visibility of a website in SERPs. The higher a website ranks in SERPs, the more traffic it will attract. And this is the main reason why webmasters will continue to battle for the top ranks by implementing various SEO tactics.

On-page/on-site optimization refers to the SEO alterations that you make on the pages of your website or blog. You're in control of these.

Off-page SEO refers to SEO alterations that you make outside of your website. Either you or visitors to your website make these alterations. So, you're not in total control of your off-page SEO.

White-hat SEO techniques refer to SEO practices that are encouraged and are totally in accordance with the stipulations of the major search engines.

Black-hat SEO techniques refers to SEO practices that are prohibited by search engines. Webmasters adopt black-hat SEO techniques in order to achieve quick results. However, search engines penalize webmasters found guilty of this by either blacklisting and demoting their websites in SERPs or removing such websites completely.

7. Backlink

This is a link on one website redirecting to another website. Backlinks are very important because Google ranks websites based on the quantity and quality of links pointing to them.

A **"no follow" link** is one that has been tagged with a special code, which instructs search engines to ignore the link and not count it as one of the links to consider when grading the site's quality.

A **"do follow" link** is one which has not been tagged with this code, and which is considered by search engines when ranking websites.

8. Link-building

This is an off-page SEO practice, which involves proactively embedding backlinks on other websites. These backlinks redirect to your own website when clicked.

Ethical link-building refers to link building practices that are in line with the guidelines laid down by the major search engines, while unethical link building involves adopting dubious means that are frowned upon by search engines.

9. Anchor text

This is the clickable text that indicates a link. In other words, it is the text you click on, which in fact is a link that redirects to another page.

10. Link-bait

A link-bait is any content or feature on a website that is interesting enough to catch people's attention. Link-baits are designed specifically to gain attention or encourage others to link to a website.

Examples of link-baits include valuable content, quality videos that reveal problem-solving information, and infographics that reveal staggering statistics

11. Page Rank

Page Rank (PR) is a measure of the quality of a web page. It is based on complex mathematical calculations that analyze the quality and quantity of backlinks to a page, among other factors. Page Rank is one of the factors that influence the ranking of a web page in SERPs.

A PR of "N/A" depicts that Google is yet to analyze a website. A PR of 0-1 depicts a new website that is of low quality. A PR of 2-4 depicts intermediate quality. A PR of 5 and above depicts high quality. Authority websites such as Wikipedia have PR of 6 to 10.

12. Alexa rank

Alexa rank is a measure of the traffic a website receives relative to other websites.

13. Algorithm update

An algorithm update is an automated massive alteration by search engines, which is aimed at checking unethical SEO practices among webmasters. Examples of popular algorithm updates are **Panda** and **Penguin**, both by Google.

During an algorithm update, websites found to have violated the regulations of search engines in some ways are either demoted in the SERPs or removed from the rankings altogether.

For example, during an update targeted at websites that have created unnatural backlinks, websites found guilty of creating such links would be demoted or de-indexed.

To protect your website from being slapped during a Google update, check Google's webmaster guidelines.

14. Social media

Social media refers to the various means of online interactions among people, in which they create, share, and exchange information and ideas in virtual communities and networks. It comprises social networking and social bookmarking.

A **social networking** site is a platform for promoting interaction among people who share similar interests, activities, backgrounds, and real life connections. Examples of social networking websites include Facebook, Twitter, LinkedIn, and Google+.

A **social bookmarking** service refers to a platform through which users store, share, organize, and manage links and bookmarks to valuable web pages and online resources. Examples of social bookmarking sites include Digg, Reddit, and Stumbleupon.

15. Article marketing

This online marketing strategy entails creating valuable and relevant articles that centre around your business or blog topic. The articles are then submitted to reputable article directories, with the aim of generating traffic and high quality backlinks for SEO.

16. Guest posting

This is another online marketing technique, which involves publishing valuable content on high quality (in terms of traffic and Google Page Rank) blogs within your niche.

The aim of guest posting is to drive traffic to your blog or website and to create high quality backlinks from other sites.

17. Traffic

This simply refers to the visits that a website or blog attracts.

18. Duplicate content

Duplicate content refers to large chunks of content that appear on more than one web page – either on the same website or on different websites.

Search engines frown at duplicate content and penalize websites found guilty of duplicating content from other websites.

Plagiarism is the practice of copying and publishing content from another web page without the approval of the owner. Plagiarized content is regarded as duplicate content by search engines.

19. PPC

PPC means **pay-per-click**, and it refers to an internet marketing strategy used to direct traffic to websites.

In PPC marketing, advertisers pay for each click on their ads, which are usually placed on SERPs or on websites that feature content related to the ads.

20. Newsletter

This refers to a series of email messages sent to your blog subscribers. Your **subscribers** are regular visitors to your blog who have opted to receive these regular messages from you. These may be updates about your blog or business, or some other valuable information. A **mailing list** is the group of email addresses to which you send your newsletter.

21. RSS Feed

RSS means **Really Simple Syndication**. It is a way of easily distributing a blog's content (such as new posts) to its regular readers without them having to visit the website.

Subscribers to an RSS feed can read the syndicated content using specialized readers that organize the content in an easy-to-read format.

22. HTML/ CSS

HTML stands for **Hypertext Markup Language**. A system of codes, it is the main computer language for creating web pages. As a blogger or internet entrepreneur, you'll need some basic knowledge of HTML.

CSS means **Cascading Style Sheet**. It is a set of coded instructions that define the semantics and architecture of a web page.

So, HTML is used to structure content, while CSS is used for formatting structured content.

23. Infographic

An infographic (information graphic) is a visual representation of some valuable information. It may contain statistical charts and other concrete illustrations.

An infographic is a fun and quick way to learn about a topic without having to read chunks of text. Infographics are commonly used as link baits.

3 Solid Reasons Why You Should Have a Blog

I've read more than enough stories by people who have made and are still making lots of cash online without having personal blogs. And many of these stories are true.

So, having a blog is not a criterion for succeeding in online business. But I will always insist that **a blog will amplify your success** because a blog is like a pedestal for any internet-based business.

I've never heard anyone claim that setting up a blog reduced his or her online income. Rather, a blog makes you even more money (this may be after some time, though). And that's why you should set up a blog from the outset.

Aside the fact that sharing your knowledge and expertise with others — through a blog — would make you feel fulfilled in a way, there are other reasons why you should have a blog. And these further explain why blogs could be real money spinners.

Here are 3 reasons why you should have a blog — regardless

of the online business you're into:

If you're a freelancer, your blog is your portfolio. If you're an affiliate marketer or information marketer, your blog is your catalog. Even if you're just sharing your knowledge, expertise, or some gist, your blog is your megaphone. So, a blog is a powerful tool for promoting any online (or offline) business.

An online entrepreneur without a blog is like a salesperson who has no showroom; he has to proactively find customers all the time. But if you have a blog, you'll attract more visitors and customers — passively. And they'll take whatever action you expect from them, even without you telling them. (And remember, the more traffic you attract, the more money you'll make.)

2. A blog builds credibility

As you may already know, I'm a freelance writer. I started making money online before setting up a blog, but I started making more money when I created a blog for my writing business than I did before doing that.

The reason isn't cryptography; I made more money simply because the blog boosted my credibility, made clients trust me and my skills the most, and portrayed me as an expert writer.

If you're an affiliate marketer, featuring quality content will compel visitors to buy the products you're promoting.

As an information marketer, you'll make more money by creating a blog that features loads of information on how visitors can benefit from your product — rather than create a static page website and slap up a sales copy that may not convert.

So, having a blog will make you even more money than you will make (or may already be making) from freelancing, information marketing, affiliate marketing, or whatever online business you're into.

3. You can earn profit through various channels

Regardless of what online business you're trying to promote with your blog, you can make more money from the same blog by featuring sponsored product reviews, displaying ads on your blog pages, selling affiliate products, and so on.

Because you can monetize a single blog in many ways, you'll continue to make money from it through other channels if your primary income channel crumbles unexpectedly.

(However, keep in mind that it would take time for your blog to start making money from multiple channels as described.)

Bottom line

So, if you're of the mindset that you can make money online or you're making the money already without your own website or blog, that's cool. Very cool.

But I would recommend that you create your own blog to boost your income and hasten your journey towards the success you've always dreamed of.

CHAPTER FOUR
CHOOSING THE RIGHT NICHE

One of the worst mistakes you can ever make in online business is to choose the wrong niche or topic for your blog. This one blunder can delay your success in online business by years – and that's if you'd succeed at all.

Your choice of a blog topic must be based on two major factors:

1. Your interest in the topic and your knowledge about it

2. The demand for information on the topic

Here's why you must choose a topic that sparks your interest...

If you blog on a topic that you really are not interested in, your zeal will quickly peter out when you start facing the harsh realities of blogging.

When you start facing discouraging challenges such as low SEO rankings, low audience engagement, low traffic, and so on, nothing can keep you going except your interest in the topic, your knowledge, and your willingness to share your experience with others.

Now, I'm not saying that you must be an expert on a topic before you can blog on it. (Of course, you can research and learn extensively about the topic and still share what you have with others.)

What I stated is that **you must have keen interest in the topic**. Don't blog on a topic simply because someone is raking in 5-6 figures from a blog on that topic (monkey see, monkey do). Don't blog on a topic because many people are also blogging on it. Don't blog on a topic because you believe you can make lots of money from it. (**Get this clear: you can make money from a blog on ANY topic.**)

Well, if you're creating your blog just to share your personal thoughts and enjoy the fun of having your writing online, you may not bother about the topic. In fact, you can pick topics at random and write on them.

But if you're blogging in order to make some income from it, you just have to choose your topic wisely.

Now, let's discuss the demand thing...

Assume you launched a bead-making blog because you love the art and want to teach it to others. You publish loads of valuable posts consistently for several months, and you adopt various blog promotion tactics.

But sadly, nobody seems to be engaging with your blog. The 2 or 3 comments you have on the blog after 6 months were placed by your close friend, your sister, and a visitor. Frustrating, isn't it?

That's what you get when you blog on a topic that only few people are interested in.

You may be knowledgeable about a topic. And you may have a burning interest to blog on it. If you're only blogging for the fun of it, and not for profit, you're free to go ahead without further planning or brainstorming.

But if your aim is to make money in the long term, then you must choose a topic that many people are interested in.

No matter how keen your interest in a topic is, you'll have that interest dampened when you seem to be the only one involved. It's like having just 2 people turning up for a speech you're to deliver at a venue that was prepared for 1000 people.

Blog topics/niches that will quickly attract a huge Nigerian audience

Having stated all the above, let me now share with you some hot blog topics/niches that will quickly attract a Nigerian audience. If you start a blog on any of these topics, chances are, you'll start making money within a short period (I didn't say a few weeks!).

Before I roll out my list, please remember that your choice of a niche must be based on your personal interest as well as demand for the information you want to share.

Although the topics in this list would quickly attract a large audience due to high demand for the related information, **you won't have a smooth sail if you don't have a natural interest in them or you don't know much about them**. Rather, in that case, I'd advise to look elsewhere and brainstorm further for a topic that will meet the two major criteria that I stated earlier.

Also, note that **this list is restricted to topics that will quickly attract a NIGERIAN audience.** If your plan is to target a global audience (probably because you can make more money that way), then stay hooked to this blog. Very soon, I'll be publishing a list of hot blog topics that will attract a global audience quickly.

Now, here's my list...

1. Small business and self-employment ideas

Because of the high rate of unemployment in Nigeria, there's a huge demand for information on how to set up a small business and become self-employed.

Whenever I browse through the business section of most Nigerian online communities and forums, I see questions like *"what business can I start with N10,000?"*, *"what business can I start with N200,000?"*, *"how can I set up my own small business"*, and so on. These questions can give you brilliant blog post ideas.

Share tips on how to start a small business, how to market it, how to manage your money, and so on. You'll quickly attract the attention of many unemployed or underemployed Nigerians. That's free information for them, and traffic for you. (More traffic = more money.)

2. Tips on how to get a job

Even though there are few of such vacant office positions in Nigeria, some never-say-die graduates would never give up on their search for office jobs. You'll easily attract the attention of such people if you share tips on how to get a job.

Share tips on how to prepare for a job interview, how to answer interview questions, how to write a great job application, how to write a killer CV, and so on.

3. Android devices and tutorials

Now, Android phones have taken over the Nigerian smartphone market (thanks to Tecno and high end brands like Samsung and Sony). You'd be amazed at the rate at which Nigerians are searching the web for information about Android phones (Tecno, especially).

Share the latest news about the Android platform, the latest Android devices in market, the rating and prices of Android devices, reviews of Android apps as well tutorials and tricks on how to do various things with an Android device. This topic will be great for you if you're tech-savvy.

4. Best deals and promo offers

Everyone loves to buy things for cheap -- and we Nigerians aren't an exception. You'll attract a huge audience if you start a blog that breaks news about discount offers, promos, and price comparisons. Although, you'll spend lots of time on research, you'll be amazed at how people will engage with your blog and at how advertisers will be queuing to buy ad space on your blog.

5. Entertainment news and celebrity gist

Personally, I dislike this niche because I think it has already been beaten into pulp by Nigerian bloggers. But the truth is, you'll always get an audience if you start a blog on the topic. But you'll need to post fresh news on a frequent basis in order to attract and retain a large audience.

6. Make money online

Well, that's exactly what this very blog is all about. Many Nigerians – employed or not – want to increase their monthly income by venturing into online business. So, anyone who shares relevant and valuable information in this regard will attract a large audience within a very short time.

Share the various ways by which people can make money online, how they can start their online businesses, how they can monetize their websites and blogs, how they can make money even without owning a website or blog, and how they can make money online using only their smartphones, among many other topics.

7. Business and investment opportunities

Due to Nigeria's unstable economy, Nigerians are always looking for ways to prepare for bad times. Today, many salary earners are on the lookout for promising investment opportunities that will boost their income. So, if you create a blog about business and investment opportunities, you'll attract a huge audience – of people who really have money (if that would be anything to go by).

Break news about latest public share offers, property for sale at cheap prices, and other investment opportunities.

8. How to travel abroad

For obvious reasons (don't ask me to explain), many Nigerians are desperately seeking to travel abroad for a better quality of living, among other motives. You'll quickly attract hundreds to thousands of these "desperadoes" if you share on your blog information that will be of help to them.

Share tips on how to secure overseas scholarships, how to secure a visa, how to choose the right overseas destinations, and so on.

9. Admissions and scholarships

Presently, there are millions of Nigerian youths seeking admission into the nation's tertiary institutions. These people are ready to implement any helpful tips they find on any blog. So, if you share information that will interest them, you'll get a huge audience.

You'll also attract undergraduates by sharing information about the latest scholarship schemes

Break the news about post UTME guidelines as published by various institutions, share tips on how to pass the UTME, share tips on how to pass the post UTME, break the news about scholarship schemes...

Monetization tip: package the post-UTME past questions and answers for various institutions into PDF format and sell them to your audience. You'll make money!

10. Free software codes and cracks

Nigerians love getting things through the easiest means possible. You'll quickly build a high traffic blog if you share software cracks and codes, free browsing APNs, links to free ebooks and software, tutorials and tricks, etc.

However, I'd advice you not to blog on this topic – for two reasons:

- Google hates blogs and websites that disclose vital information illegally. So, your blog will most likely be denied approval for Adsense.
- Advertisers don't like to be associated with sites that ravish others' privacies. So, you won't make money from selling ad space, even if you have a massive audience.

Other promising niches

11. Jokes

12. Football gist

13. Blogging tips

14. Fashion

15. Health and beauty tips

But there's more money in targeting a global audience

Yes, you're likely to make more money from your blog in the long term if you target a global audience rather than staying local. And there are reasons for this.

Firstly, most Nigerian internet users don't engage with ads. So, you may not really get much Adsense clicks as to fetch you good money.

Secondly, most Nigerian internet users browse the web with their mobile devices. And since Adsense ads display poorly on mobile browsers, you won't attract much clicks.

Thirdly, because buying products online is still very new in Nigeria, you won't be able to make money from affiliate marketing, which is a real money spinner and the biggest source of income for many bloggers.

Fourthly, Nigerians are very reluctant to part with their money. Though you can have all their loyalty as long as you offer free information, most of them won't buy your product when you pitch them – even if you try hard to convince them of its benefits.

So, I, personally, prefer to target a global audience unless I'm very sure of a huge Nigerian audience, and I'm ready to overlook those monetization methods that won't work on a blog targeted at Nigerians.

Which niches should you choose for a global audience?

Well, the truth is, any niche or topic can fetch you good money from an international audience if you play your cards right.

But the following niches are particularly lucrative:

- Health
- Small business
- Technology
- Green living
- Personal finance
- Pet care

PS. Niches like health and technology comprise several sub-topics. A proven success tip is to choose one sub-topic (skin health, mental health, health tips for the pregnant, kids health, etc. – under the health niche) and focus on it. Specificity rocks! If you choose a niche that is too generic, you're more likely to fail.

So, what's next?

After choosing a suitable niche, there's another step you MUST take if you really hope to build a high traffic blog. And that's KEYWORD RESEARCH. It's a vital part of any successful online business, and it could make or mar your blog. You'll learn more about it later on.

CHAPTER FIVE

HOW TO CREATE A BLOG USING BLOGGER (A STEP-BY-STEP GUIDE)?

Even though there are many blogging platforms available, Google's **Blogger** (also known as Blogspot) and **Wordpress** are by far the most popular platforms used by bloggers.

If you're new to blogging, you can start with Blogger because it's free and very easy to use. But I strongly recommend that you use WordPress because it's far, far better than Blogger.

To learn how to set up your blog on WordPress, read the detailed tutorial I have published on my blog. Just copy the following link into your browser to access the post: http://webincomeplus.com/how-to-set-up-a-self-hostedwordpress-blog-in-thirty-minutes-or-less/

Since it doesn't hurt to have the knowledge, I want to walk you through the simple process of setting up your new blog on Blogger. Just follow the following steps:

Setting up the blog

1. Visit www.blogger.com.

2. If you already have an account with Google (such as a Gmail account), enter your email and password in the columns provided.

3. If you don't have a Google account, click the red **"sign up"** button (top right) to

register an account first.

4. On the **Confirm your profile** page, you'll see two tabs. Click on the one by the right (**Create a limited Blogger profile**). An empty column will pop up under for your display name. In this column, enter the name you'd like to be displayed on your blog and on your posts. (You can use your real name or a pseudonym.)

5. Check the **"feature announcements"** box.

6. Click **"continue to Blogger"**. (You'll be taken to the next page.)

7. On the next page (**Your Name's Blogs**), click on **"New blog"**.

8. In the spaces provided, enter the title of your new blog and your preferred URL address.

9. Choose a template from the displayed options to start with

10. Hit the **"Create blog"** button.

And that's it! You now have your new blog. And you can start blogging right away.

Getting started

Click on the **"start blogging"** link, and you'll be taken to the **Overview** page.

On the left side of this page, there is a menu with a list of tabs -- Overview, Posts, Pages, Comments, etc.

Before I explain how to publish a new post, let me tell you more about these tabs:

- **Overview:** displays summarized information about your blog - such as number of page views, comments, etc.

- **Posts:** displays your published posts as well as those saved as draft.
- **Pages:** displays your blog's stand-alone pages -- such as **About** page, **Contact** page, etc.
- **Comments:** displays the comments left by readers on your blog posts.
- **Google+:** displays your Google+ profile (if you have set it up).
- **Stats:** displays vital statistics about your blog, including information about your traffic sources, audience, posts, etc.
- **Earnings:** displays your Google Adsense earnings (after you've set up Adsense for your blog). Don't tamper with this for now.
- **Layout:** displays your blog's layout (you can modify this as you wish).
- **Template:** displays your blog's template.

Publishing your posts

To publish a new post on your blog, follow these steps:

1. Click the **"New post"** button (top left). (You'll be taken to another page, on which you'll write your post title and body.)
2. Enter the topic of your blog post in the **"Post title"** field.
3. Write your post body in the large space created.
4. Using the appropriate buttons at the top of the large area, format your text (bold, underline, or italicize) and add links or images (if you have any).
5. See the **"post settings"** tab by the right. Under it, you'll see the following:

- **Labels:** Enter a category for your blog post
- **Schedule:** Choose **"automatic"** to publish the post instantly.

Or set another date and time of your choice (past or future)

- **Permalink:** Set the URL for your post. (Choose **"custom permalink"** to change it to anything you prefer.)
- **Location:** State your location (not necessary)
- **Options:** Specify if you want to allow your readers to leave comments on the post.

Using the appropriate buttons by the top right, you can publish the post to send it live, preview it before publishing, or save it for later editing and publishing. If you're ready to see your post live, hit the **"publish"** button.

Now, following the steps listed in this post, set up your new blog, and let me see what you've got.

Again, I strongly recommend that you start your blogging on WordPress, because even if you start with Blogger, you'll have to move to WordPress later. So, to learn how to set up your blog on WordPress, copy the following link into your browser to access the detailed tutorial on WordPress blog setup: <u>http://webincomeplus.com/how-to-set-up-a-self-hostedwordpress-blog-in-thirty-minutes-or-less/</u>

Keyword Research: The Ultimate Guide to Finding Lucrative Keywords

If you've set up a blog for your internet business, it would rarely thrive if you're not getting organic traffic from search engines.

Yes, you may have thousands of social media followers who follow your link each time you publish a new blog post. And you may have lots of referral visits each time you post an excerpt of your latest article on Nairaland (which, to me is a questionable strategy).

Truth is, these strategies won't bring a steady flow of traffic.

If you're not given to publishing new and intriguing posts every day (as required by the entertainment niche), the best you'll get is a traffic surge each time you publish a new post. And that traffic would dwindle down to unit numbers until you publish a new post again.

But if you're blogging in other niches, or you're unable to publish new posts daily, then you won't be able to attract appreciable traffic consistently – except you rank in Google for your target keywords.

Only by implementing proven SEO tactics (we'll be discussing this in detail in the next post) can you have your blog's pages ranking high in Google and attracting lots of visits consistently – even if you don't publish new posts regularly. So, leveraging the power of Google is a surefire way to drive traffic to your blog.

Now, look at the picture below. It is a snapshot of the Google Analytics traffic report for one of my blogs (not Web Income Plus, but I won't disclose the details of the blog – for certain reasons).

The chart shows the number of visits to the blog recorded daily between July 1 and July 23, 2013. Within the period, the blog attracted 1,025 visits.

Here's an account of the number of visits on selected days within the period (as gotten from the report).

- July 1 - 14 visits
- July 5 - 36 visits
- July 11 - 70 visits
- July 14 - 27 visits
- July 16 - 95 visits

- July 23 - 54 visits

But could you believe that the last time I published a post on the blog was April 29, 2013? Yet, I could still get 1,025 visits after almost two months. It's interesting, right?

Yes, the number of daily visits isn't steady. But the fact is, I never made any effort to attract these visits except for publishing the posts in the first place.

And it may even interest you that the blog was set up on April 10, 2013, and it had just 12 posts (most of which are less than 200 words long) as at the time I took the snapshot shown above. The blog is targeted at a Nigerian audience. So, almost all the visitors to the blog are in Nigeria.

Below is another snapshot showing the traffic sources for the blog. That is, an account of where the 1,025 visits came from.

The report reveals that 68.2% of the visits (699 visits) came from search engines (Google), 7.2% (74 visits) came as referral visits from another blog I own, and the remaining 24.6% (252 visits) were direct visits (I'm still wondering why some people keep visiting the blog even when I've not updated it in a long time).

So, Google sent about 700 visitors to my blog while I abandoned it for almost 2 months.

Now, fast forward to October 2013, the blog's traffic has grown to an average of 1000+ visitors per day. I had added 14 more posts, though.

Below is a snapshot of the traffic report for the same blog for the period between October 11 – November 10, 2013.

Aside that the traffic grew by over 1,500% between July and November, it is now somewhat steadier than what obtained in the previous months.

Again, below is a snapshot showing the traffic sources for the blog within the same period.

As shown, Google sent me 29,204 visits within the period. That is 83.5% of the total traffic. The truth is, I'm still as lazy as before; I update the blog at irregular intervals. Yet, it keeps attracting thousands of visitors. I'm sure you're now wondering how I managed to achieve this.

Well, the answer is simple: keyword research.

I simply figured out the keywords that people (Nigerians) were using to search Google for the information I share on the blog. Then I optimized my post for these keywords.

After some weeks, the posts showed up on Google's front page for the keywords I optimized them for. And that was how the traffic kept coming.

If a 6-month old blog could start attracting 1000+ daily visits with just 26 posts, you can guess what would happen when I publish up to 70 posts.

I'm sure you'd like to achieve the same. I mean, you'd like your blog to attract massive traffic steadily. (Remember, more traffic = more money.)

Now, let me teach you how to find keywords that will drive traffic to your blog even when you're not publishing new posts frequently.

Actually, I use a popular tool known as the **Google**

Keyword Planner. This is great tool by Google made for keyword research.

I have used the Google Keyword Planner, and I found it to be very good – far better than any other keyword tool you can find (my opinion.)

To use the Google Keyword Planner, follow the steps below:

1. Visit **http://adwords.google.com** and login using your Google Account details (enter your Gmail username and password if you use Gmail). If you don't have a Gmail account, click the **"sign up"** button to start your registration.

2. Follow the steps in the registration process and provide the required answers. Be sure to complete your registration.

3. You can either click the link on the registration success page to access your Adwords account, or open **http://adwords.google.com** again to enter your username and password.

4. In the green menu bar displayed, click on **"Tools and analysis"** and select **"Keyword Planner"** from the dropdown menu list. Below is a snapshot of the Keyword Planner page:

5. On the Keyword Planner page, click **"Search for keyword and ad group ideas."** (You have no business with the other two options; ignore them.)

6.   In the dropdown box, enter your main blog topic in the column for **"Your product or service."** For example, if you're planning to blog about Nigerian movies, enter *"nigerian movies."* (You have no business with the "landing page" and "product category" columns; ignore them.)

7.   In the **"Targeting"** section, choose Nigeria (this should be the default value) if you're targeting a Nigerian audience. In fact, you can target Lagos only, or Abuja only, in case you're targeting only readers in those cities. If you're targeting a global audience, click **"Remove all"** at the upper right corner of the box. Click outside the box to save your settings.

8.   In the **"Customize your search"** section, click the **"Keyword filters"** box, and set the **"Average monthly searches"** to greater than 100 or 50. (Any keyword that attracts less than that is useless – in my opinion.) Ignore the **"Average CPC"** box.

9.   Click the **"Include or exclude"** box, enter your keywords (*"nigerian movies"* in our example) in the **"include terms"** box, and ignore the **"Exclude terms"** box. Below is what you should have after clicking out of the box:

10.   Click the **"Get ideas"** button, and wait for the results.

11.   In the results page, click the **"Keyword ideas"** tab, and wait again.

12.   The next page will display a list of keywords that you should target. Below is a snapshot of what I got after hitting the

"Keyword ideas" tab:

The results page displays keywords ideas, average monthly searches, competition, and average CPC values (you have no business with the average CPC values).

You have better chances of ranking quickly for low competition keywords than you have for medium and high competition keywords. So, you can start with the low competition keywords, but you should target all keywords, except those that are not in line with your topic.

Here are the 15 keywords I got:

- *nigerian movies download*
- *watch free nigerian movies online*
- *download nigerian movies*
- *nigerian movies free download*
- *latest nigerian movies*
- *free nigerian movies download • watch nigerian movies online*
- *download free nigerian movies*
- *watch free nigerian movies*
- *free nigerian movies*
- *nigerian movies on youtube*
- *nigerian movies online*
- *nigerian movies youtube*
- *youtube nigerian movies*

- *watch nigerian movies*

So, if you have a blog about Nigerian movies, you should optimize your blog posts for these keywords. If you do, chances are high that you'll rank for them quickly, and you'll generate lots of traffic from Google.

Here's another thing you should keep in mind: the longer a keyword, the higher your chances of ranking high for it. That is, you have a brighter chance of ranking high for *"watch free nigerian movies online"* than for *"watch nigerian movies."* (This is not always the case, though. So, try to optimize for all keywords that come your way. But you can stay clear of keyword phrases that contain just 2 words – e.g. "Nigerian movies.")

In the next lesson, you'll learn how to optimize your blog posts for your target keywords.

PS: You'll need a very good internet connection to use the Google Keyword Planner. And note that you cannot conduct keyword research using a mobile phone

CHAPTER SIX

A BEGINNERS' GUIDE TO SEO (SEARCH ENGINE OPTIMIZATION)

I want you to get something very clearly: **Blogging isn't just about generating massive traffic; it's about generating traffic that will help you actualize your dream – to make money online.**

Tell me, of what use is a blog that attracts 1,000 visitors per day when you're not making money from that traffic? It's of NO use because generating traffic isn't your ultimate goal. Making real cash is.

Now, I'm not saying you shouldn't work towards attracting lots of visitors. You should. In fact, the more visitors your blog attracts, the more money you're likely to make. But what I'm saying is that traffic, in itself, isn't an end; it's a means to a more important end (to make money). You get it now?

OK, let me bring an instance.

Assume you're a freelance writer (like me), and you've set up a blog with the aim of attracting quality clients.

On your blog, you share high quality and interesting information on how to write killer articles and other pieces of content. Of course, you want potential clients to see those posts and say *"Oh, this guy must be a very good writer. I'm hiring him right away."*

After some time, your blog starts to rank high in Google for keyword phrases like *"how to write a good article"* and *"how to optimize your posts."*

Because of these high rankings, your traffic increases to about 300 visits per day. Of course, such a result would make you happy. And really, you're generating traffic, which means your chances of attracting quality clients through your blog are getting higher (on paper).

But don't be surprised if no client contacts you for a writing gig after several months of generating decent traffic on your blog. I know that's disastrous. **But that's what will happen.** You know why? I'll tell you...

It's not because your content isn't interesting or relevant enough. It's not because your blog is poorly designed. And it's not because your visitors don't want to hire a Nigerian. It's because you're not attracting the right visitors. Period.

Granted, you're attracting many visitors on a daily basis, and one would expect that the high quality information you share on your blog would help you convert many readers into clients – those long term, high paying clients that you really need.

But those clients aren't visiting your blog because you're not using your content to attract them. If you're really doing this, you don't even need to generate as much as 200 daily visits before you'll get choked with the high paying writing assignments you always wanted.

At this point, let me ask you a question.

Which category of people do you think would be searching Google for those keywords your blog is ranking for? I mean, keyword phrases like *"how to write a good a good article"* and *"how to optimize your posts."*

Those keywords are used by people who are either bloggers or writers themselves, but need additional tips on how to create or optimize their content correctly. These are not people looking to hire a freelance writer. They can write, too. It's just that they need some helpful tips.

So, how can such a blog attract a single client when the daily visitors are those who are not ready to hire you? You get it now?

To attract clients (on such a blog), you need to target keywords like the following:

- *"hire freelance writer"*
- *"hire blog writer"*
- *"article writing services"*
- *"cheap article writer"*

These are the queries that people use to search Google when they're looking for freelance writers to hire. And if your major reason for blogging is to attract clients, these are the keywords you should be targeting.

So, this is the bottom line: **To make money online, you need to publish content that will attract the kind of visitors who will give help you achieve that goal.**

This process of optimizing your blog's content for search engines by targeting keywords (search queries) used by your target audience is known as SEO (Search Engine Optimization).

In more detail, what is SEO?

SEO is a website or blog promotion technique that involves

strategically embedding <u>lucrative keywords</u> within your content. This is with the aim that your blog should show up prominently in search engine results when users search the web with queries matching those keywords you're targeting.

The result of these efforts is increased traffic, since most visitors are more likely to click on the links that rank highest in search result pages.

So, if you're blogging about Nigerian movies, for instance, you'll attract lots of traffic if you target keywords that Nigerians are using to search for movies online, and you're highly ranked in search result pages for those keywords.

(To understand how to figure out which keywords your target audience are using to search the web, see the previous lesson.)

There are two major categories of SEO practices

As stated earlier, search engine optimization involves a number of practices that are aimed at improving the visibility of your website or blog in search engine result pages. These practices can be classified into two main categories:

- On-page SEO
- Off-page SEO

What are on-page SEO strategies?

These SEO practices are implemented right on the pages of your website or blog. You have absolute control over on-page SEO, and you'll be held responsible by search engines for any on-page SEO malpractices detected on your website or blog.

On-page SEO may be all that you need to have your web pages or blog posts ranking highly in Google for your target keywords – provided you're targeting low competition keywords.

The following is a list of on-page SEO strategies that you should implement on your web pages for improved search engine visibility:

- Including your main keyword phrase in your blog's main title
- Including your main keyword phrase in your blog's description
-

    Including your target keywords (secondary) in the title and description of your blog posts
- Using search engine-friendly URL structures that allow you to embed your target keywords within your URLs
- Using your target keywords as alt tags for your images
- Linking the pages of your website or blog together (internal linking)
- Including your target keywords in the body of your content – preferably within the first few lines
- Including your keywords within your content's subtitles (H1 and H2 tags)

What are off-page SEO strategies?

These SEO practices are implemented on other blogs or websites. Majorly, off-page SEO involves building backlinks that redirect to your website or blog.

Off-page SEO has more effect on your search engine rankings because search engines see links pointing to your website or blog (from other websites or blogs) as a "vote of confidence" from those blogs.

So, the more backlinks you have pointing to your web pages, the more search engines will trust your site, and the higher you'll rank for your target keywords.

(We'll discuss link-building, the main off-page SEO strategy, in more detail later on.)

What are "White-hat" and "Black-hat" SEO practices?

White-hat or ethical SEO practices are those SEO strategies (on-page and off-page) that are in line with the guidelines and regulations laid down by the major search engines (Google, Yahoo, and Bing).

All the on-page SEO strategies listed above are white-hat techniques, and you'll never have any problems with search engines if you implement them correctly.

To read more about the ethical SEO guidelines for webmasters, read Google's SEO guidelines for webmasters. You can find this by searching Google with the query, *"Google Webmaster Guidelines."* Black-hat or unethical SEO techniques refer to practices that go against the guidelines of ethical SEO. These techniques are aimed majorly at deceiving search engines. Examples include the following:

- **Keyword stuffing:** unnecessary repetition of your target keywords within your content
- **Paid links:** buying backlinks (usually low-quality links) from other websites
- **Reciprocal links:** "I link to you and you link back to

me" arrangements

- **Link farming:** building a network of blogs or websites and linking them together to form a network
- **Automated links:** building backlinks with software and spambots
- **Invisible text:** adding keyword-laden text that blends with your background colour so that readers cannot see them

While black-hat SEO techniques may bring quick results, these results are often short-lived because your website or blog will be temporarily or permanently banned or penalized once the search engines detect some foul play.

Bottom line

Now, I believe you've learned the basics of SEO as well as proven SEO tactics that should suffice if you implement them correctly.

To further understand SEO and how it works, you can read the following online authoritative and elaborate resources on the topic:

- MOZ: The Beginners' Guide to SEO
- Wikipedia: Search Engine Optimization

Practical SEO: How to Optimize Your Blog Posts for Continuous Traffic

Some bloggers would tell you to write on any topic that comes to your mind, since blogging is a way of sharing your knowledge and expressing your ideas. But I beg to disagree.

If you want to make money from your blog, you have to write on things that people (your target audience, I mean) really want to read – not on just anything.

Generating traffic is what boosts your income as a blogger, and only by sharing what your readers really want can you achieve that.

To find out what your target audience wants to read isn't difficult. Simply do some keyword research, and you'll get tons of topic ideas for your blog posts. If you've been reading this ebook from its very beginning, I expect you to have understood how to do this. If you've not, go back to the lesson on keyword research.

After getting a list of lucrative keywords, you have to optimize your blog posts for them. In this lesson, I'll be teaching you how to strategically optimize your blog posts so that they'll show up in search engine results when people search for information using queries that match your target keywords.

Keep in mind that optimizing a post for search engines isn't as difficult or as complex as many people think. Just follow the few steps you're about to learn, and you'll get your desired results.

Quality content comes first...

As a blogger, providing your readers with unique, valuable, and authentic information should be your utmost motive.

Even if you're generating high traffic, you still won't make money if your visitors don't find your content useful. Only when they love your content would they take any action that will fetch you some cash.

So, never compromise on the quality of the information you

share on your blog. Make sure each new post you publish solves a problem, answers a question, or shares some rare information.

With the above in mind, let's now discuss the steps involved in optimizing a blog post.

1. Insert your keyword in the post title

Having your target keyword within the topic of your blog post is a very powerful on-page SEO tactic. It helps your post rank above many others written on the same topic but without the keyword in their titles.

Even if you've crafted your topic before writing your post, it is necessary for you to adjust it to include your target keyword. For example, if your target keyword is *"used cars in Nigeria"*, a well optimized topic would be *"How to buy **used cars in Nigeria."***

Even if you personally prefer a title like *"How to buy second-hand cars in Nigeria"*, you should adjust it to include your target keyword (which, of course, is the phrase people are using to search Google for information on buying new cars in Nigeria).

If you're using Blogger, this step is very simple and straightforward (just do as explained). But if you're using Wordpress, you'll need to install an SEO plugin (like the All-in-One SEO Pack or the Wordpress SEO plugin by Yoast), and enter your optimized title both in the title column for the post and that of the plugin.

2. Insert your keyword in the page description

A description is a brief summary of the information

contained in your blog post. Though it doesn't really work for SEO, adding a compelling description to your post helps entice readers to click on it in search engine results or social media pages.

When writing your description, include your target keyword. Make it blend well with the rest of the summary (this may difficult with some keywords, but always try to work out a readable description).

In Blogger, you'll find the **"search description"** tab by the right when you're writing a new post. Enter your description here.

If you're using Wordpress, enter your description in the **"description"** field of your SEO plugin.

3. Embed your keyword within the permalink

Simply put, the permalink is the URL of your blog post. Inserting your keyword in the permalink is a proven SEO game-changer. So, never skip it.

Both Blogger and Wordpress allow you to change a post's permalink to whatever you like. If you use Blogger, click the **"Permalink"** tab by the right and choose **"Custom permalink."** Then enter your desired permalink structure. I'd advise that you limit this to your keyword only and separate each word with a hyphen.

So, if you're targeting the keyword *"used cars in Nigeria"*, just enter ***"used-cars-in-nigeria"*** as your custom permalink.

Before you can customize your permalink effectively in Wordpress, ensure that you've set an SEO-friendly permalink structure.

(Dashboard >> Settings >> Permalinks >> Post name >> Save changes) Then click the **"edit"** button next to the URL right under the post title field and enter your desired permalink.

4. Use your keyword in the first line or paragraph

If possible, use your target keyword within the first line (or paragraph) of your post. Some experts claim that this tip works for SEO, but I've gotten great results without implementing it. So, I opine that its impact on SEO is very minimal, if it has any at all.

5. Use your keyword in the alt text

If you're adding an image to your blog post, use your keyword within the image's alt text. This also has minimal impact on the post's ranking, but it has a more powerful impact in image search rankings.

So, if you want your image to show up when people search for images using your target keyword, simply implement this tip.

Here's a warning…

Never distort your keyword in any way. If your keyword is *"used cars Nigeria"*, don't change it to something like *"used cars in Nigeria"* or *"Nigerian used cars"* because you think it is better that way. Use your keywords exactly as the keyword tool revealed them. If you distort them, you may not get the expected results.

On a final note…

When reading other blogs, you may come across additional

tips that I did not mention here.

Some bloggers would tell you to add your keyword within the subtitles in your post, repeat your keyword in every paragraph, keep your keyword in bold, and so on. But the truth is, all these tactics don't work anymore! Yes, they worked at some time in the past, but SEO is an ever-changing game.

If you really want your posts to show on Google, the few tips in this post – especially the first three – would help you achieve that. With these simple tips, I've ranked several posts on Google's first page for different keywords. And you'll get the same results too, provided you're targeting the right keywords.

PS. Because SEO is an ever-changing game, the tactics I revealed in this lesson may lose their effectiveness in the future. Always read authoritative SEO blogs to keep abreast of latest trends in the SEO world

CHAPTER SEVEN

8 FOOLPROOF TIPS FOR ATTRACTING TRAFFIC TO YOUR BLOG POSTS

Visitors won't flow to your blog by osmosis. You have to proactively adopt smart measures to attract them. If you slap up a few articles and sit back expecting the traffic to come, you're in for big disappointment and frustration. (And this is why many bloggers quit early.)

So, how can you attract traffic to each new blog post you publish? That's exactly what I'll be teaching you here.

I won't stop telling you this...

Quality content is what makes the difference between a blog that merely attracts traffic and a blog that really makes money.

You may be attracting thousands of visitors, but you won't make money if the average visitor "bounces off" your blog within 10 seconds after landing on it.

But if you offer content that is helpful, problem-solving, valuable, and unique, you'll compel visitors to stay longer on your blog and absorb your content. And aside engaging with your content, they'll click on your ads, buy through your affiliate links, hire your freelance services, buy ad space on your blog, and take whatever action that would fetch you money.

So, quality content is the biggie when it comes to blogging and online business. It's king, like the popular saying goes (*"Content is king."*) And reality agrees with that.

With the above in mind, let's now look at some proven tactics for attracting quality traffic to your blog posts.

1. Killer headlines work like magic

Whether or not a reader would feel eager to go through your post hinges largely on your headline. Your headline should be crafted in a way that triggers curiosity in the mind of the reader. This way, anyone would feel compelled to check it out.

However, avoid a headline that sounds too good to be true or that makes a promise you cannot deliver on. Only few things could be more annoying to readers than this.

2. Blast them off on social media

After publishing a new post on your blog, publish it on your social media profiles as well. With your Facebook and Twitter accounts, spread word of your new article by posting its URL. Your friends, relatives, and colleagues would get to see the link and follow it to your blog. And they'll share with their own friends and colleagues, too.

But if your headline isn't catchy or your content isn't valuable and interesting, people won't read it, let alone share it

3. Ask… and it shall be given unto you

People are busy. They don't have the time to share your post after reading it. They have other things begging for their attention. But they're ready to do anything you ask for as a way of rewarding you for the quality information you offered.

So, if you ask readers to help you share your post with others via social media, they'll readily do that. That's the power of asking. If you don't ask, they won't share – even though it's something they can do easily.

One important thing you should do, however, is to make it easy for your readers to share your post. Most readers won't share your post if they would have to open new browser tabs for that. So, add the various social media share one-click share buttons to your posts. They make sharing pretty easier.

4. Social bookmarking works like wild

You can generate massive traffic by sharing your new posts on social bookmarking sites like Reddit, Digg, Stumbleupon, and so on. These sites allow you to post links to recommended web pages. If your headline is catchy enough, you'll attract tons of clicks to your link (and ultimately, lots of readers to your blog).

If those who read your post found it really valuable and helpful, your link would attract many votes. Depending on the number of such votes, your link may just find its way to the home page (of the social bookmarking site). If this happens, your blog would host hundreds to thousands of visitors.

5. Don't overlook forum marketing (as others are doing)

Forum marketing simply involves using a forum to drive traffic to your blog. After publishing a new blog post, start a forum thread on the same topic. Share a summary of your article and add a link to the blog post.

The more you engage with others on the forum thread and share your knowledge of the topic with them, the more they'll follow the link to read your blog post. This tactic works like wild.

6. Blog commenting isn't dead

You can also get a decent amount of traffic from other blogs. After publishing a new post, use Google to find other blog posts on the same topic. Post a detailed, valuable comment on the blog, and add that you just published a post on the same topic that readers would find equally helpful. Then add the link to the blog post.

This strategy works best if you're one of the first commentators on the blog post you found. The earlier you post your comment, the higher up in the page (and more visible) it will be.

7. Borrow traffic from high traffic blogs

After publishing a series of related posts on your blog, find high traffic blogs within your niche that accept guest posts. Write a valuable and informative post and strategically include links to your blog posts (within the guest post). The more valuable your guest post is, the more traffic it would send to your blog.

Guest posting is a real traffic magnet. But many bloggers are just too lazy to utilize it to their advantage. Don't be like them – if you really want traffic.

8. SEO is the **REAL DEAL!**

While most of the strategies I've shared so far would only generate traffic for a short term, SEO would continue to bring you traffic for as long as your content remains relevant. So, if you want your blog posts to generate steady traffic for years to come, optimize them for the search engines.

People will continue to use search engines for as long as they exist, and search engines would always present posts and pages that are most relevant to people's queries. So, do some extensive keyword research before writing your blog posts and optimize them strategically before hitting the "publish" button. This way, you'll rank your posts high in search engine results and ultimately attract traffic to your blog.

To learn how to research for lucrative keywords and optimize your blog posts for them, refer to the lesson on keyword research and the previous lesson.

The more traffic you generate on your blog, the brighter your chances of making money. If you take your online business more seriously and implement these strategies religiously, you'll start getting your desired results very soon.

CHAPTER EIGHT

ETHICAL LINK BUILDING: ALL YOU NEED TO KNOW

Earlier on, I explained the importance of keyword research and how to conduct it. I also explained the concept of on-page SEO and how to implement it on your blog posts.

Here, I'll be discussing the main task that off-page SEO involves – link building.

In case you don't know what the terms *"keyword research"*, *"on-page SEO"*, and *"off-page SEO"* mean, refer to the previous lessons get full understanding of them:

Now, let's discuss the main topic, which is link building.

After researching for lucrative keywords and optimizing your blog posts for them, you'll most likely have your blog ranking for your target keywords – provided you avoided high competition keywords.

But there are times when your efforts still won't produce the desired results. I mean, sometimes, your blog won't rank as you expected after targeting and optimizing your post for particular low competition keyword phrase.

And there are times when your blog ranks well for your target keyword, but soon starts to go down gradually until you can no longer find it on the first results page.

Both instances could be frustrating. Very frustrating.

The cause of the problem in both cases is the same – your blog doesn't have enough "authority" to rank well for the keyword phrase. So, it cannot compete with the big sites that are sitting on top of the search result rankings for that keyword phrase. And if it finds its way among them for some time, they quickly send it back to down below.

Now, what is this authority thing?

You see, aside ranking sites based on their relevance to the keyword phrases used in search queries, Google also uses a concept known as "domain authority" to rank sites.

The domain authority of a blog can simply be defined as the measure of the blog's quality and credibility. How does Google estimate this? **Simply by looking at the number of quality links that are pointing back to the blog from other blogs or websites.** You get it now?

So, even if you've optimized your post well for a low competition keyword, some websites and blogs may still outrank yours if they have higher domain authority than your blog. But this rarely happens if you target long-tail keywords with very low competition.

Now, why does Google rank websites based on backlinks? The answer is, **Google considers a backlink pointing to your blog from another blog or website as a vote of confidence and trust from that blog.** And the higher the domain authority of the blog or website linking to you, the higher the quality of the link itself.

So, the higher the number (and quality) of backlinks pointing to your blog from other blogs and websites, the higher your blog's domain authority becomes. And the stronger your chances of ranking for medium to high competition keywords as well as keeping your position in the rankings for a long time.

What is ethical link building?

Ethical (or "white-hat") link building simply refers to creating backlinks in ways that are organic ("natural") and that involve no manipulations or shortcuts. Search engines hate unnatural links and they penalize websites and blogs found to be associated with them.

So, when you create backlinks for your blog, ensure that you do not violate any of the link building guidelines laid down by the major search engines.

Here are 4 ways to create backlinks that won't get your blog penalized in the long run:

1. Quality content

If you're too lazy (or too stingy) to create and publish valuable and unique content on your blog, then you have no business with blogging or online business in general.

Quality content is one of the major factors that matter in online business – in case you didn't know before now.

By publishing quality content on your blog that readers find very helpful and informative, you'll attract lots of backlinks from other websites and blogs. I mean, other people who found your content helpful would link to it from their own blogs. This is the easiest (and most ethical) way to generate quality backlinks.

2. Guest posting

Aside helping you attract traffic from other blogs, guest posting is a powerful link building strategy. Virtually all blogs would give you the chance to add a link or two to your blog within your guest post.

So, if you're looking to create high quality backlinks, publish guest posts on authority blogs within your niche.

3. Article marketing

This involves publishing articles on article directories such as Ezine articles. These directories allow you to place one or two links within the author bio section of your article, thereby sending links to your blog.

Many bloggers would tell you that article marketing is dead and no longer works for link building. But I beg to disagree. Let me share this with you:

Sometimes in February 2013, a client of mine who just set up a new blog wanted the blog to rank on Google's front page for his main target keyword. Because the domain name included the target keyword, I was optimistic that the blog would rank well once we published some articles.

But that wasn't to be. The blog didn't even get to the third page of Google's results for the target keyword. For 2-3 weeks after we published a series of long, high quality, well-optimized articles, the blog ranked between positions 31 and 33.

I had to do something fast. Then I thought of article marketing. I explained the whole concept to the client, and we both agreed that I'll write 15 articles and have them published them on article directories (an article to one directory). I did this over a period of one month.

After I published 7 out of the 15 articles, the blog jumped

up to the 11th position. After I published 9 articles, the blog ranked 10th. After the last article went live, the blog moved up to the 8th position. Mission accomplished – thanks to article marketing.

So who says article marketing is dead? It's still alive. And it still works – magically!

During some algorithm updates that happened in the past, most of the popular article directories lost their rankings in Google because webmasters were using them to create spammy links. Yes, this happened, and it's the reason why most webmasters think that article directories have lost all their relevance. But in reality, they only lost their rankings, not their authority, and not their Page Rank values.

4. Blog commenting

You can also create backlinks by leaving helpful comments on other people's blog posts. Because the comment form allows you to leave your blog address, each comment you leave automatically includes a backlink to your blog.

But don't abuse this technique by leaving silly comments like *"nice post"* or *"thanks."* Doing this clearly shows that you're more interested in creating a backlink than anything else. It annoys most bloggers, and it gets your comment trashed.

So, when you leave comments on other blogs, leave detailed comments that show you really read the post.

Conclusion

While there are many other link-building techniques, I'd advise you to stick with only these four. Reciprocal backlinking (exchanging backlinks) is frowned upon by search engines. Automated backlinking (generating links with software) creates tons of spammy backlinks that may get you quick results, but will eventually leave you badly burnt in the long term.

Once again, stick with only the four link building tactics I shared here, and you'll get good, long-term results.

CHAPTER NINE

HOW TO QUICKLY INCREASE YOUR BLOG'S PROFIT POTENTIAL

Going by the headline of this post, you may be expecting me to unleash some magical tricks here that will turn your blog into an ATM machine overnight. But the truth is, I don't know even one of such tricks myself. In fact, I doubt if such tricks exist.

You see, my friend, online business is serious business. And there are no shortcuts to attaining success in it. So, if I tell you that your blog can become a money-spinner "very soon," I don't mean tomorrow. I don't mean next week. And I don't mean next month.

Really, what I mean is "within the shortest time possible." This could be as short as 3-6 months or as long as 3-6 years. (I know you hate the "3-6 years" part, but don't go crazy. You'd only have to wait that long if you're not taking your online business seriously.)

Here, I'm giving you one secret (maybe it's not a secret, anyway) that will help you start making money from your online business as soonest as possible.

And that secret is...

CONSISTENCY

That is, you need to be consistent in publishing high quality posts that are well optimized for search engines, and in promoting your blog through link building and other techniques. That's all!

Consistency makes all the difference between a successful blogger and one struggling to get results. And lack of consistency is one major reason why most people fail at blogging and think online business is just another shitty hoax. So, if you want to make money from online business at all, consistency is key.

Try to publish at least 3 new posts each week. If you can publish more, that's better. But you must stick with a number that you can keep up with. Publishing 6 posts this week and only one next week is just silly. So, publish a fixed number of posts per week – and on fixed days of the week. (And remember, quality is what matters most. Never publish crap!)

You must be consistent in promoting your blog as well. Each time you publish a new post, spread word of it using the traffic generation techniques I shared earlier.

Also, build backlinks consistently. (Your aim here is to rank well for your target keywords and thereby generate traffic steadily from the search engines.) Submit each new post to social bookmarking sites like Reddit, Digg, Stumbleupon, and so on. Leave comments on at least 3 blogs per day. Publish one guest post every 1 or 2 weeks. And publish an article on an article submission site every 2 weeks.

So, to start making money from your blog as soonest as possible, keep up doing the following, AT LEAST:

- Publish 3 articles on your blog weekly
- Promote each blog post on social media
- Submit each blog post to social bookmarking sites
- Leave comments on 3 other blogs daily

- Publish guest posts every two weeks
- Submit articles to article directories every two weeks

If you're too lazy to complete these tasks consistently, then you'll either spend years trying to make money from your blog or leave online business out of frustration. So, you'd better quit now.

But if you really want to build a very profitable blog, complete these tasks consistently, and you'd see great results within few months.

What results should you expect from these efforts?

Huge traffic. Not just traffic that will land on your site and "bounce." I mean traffic that will click your ads if you're doing Google Adsense, traffic that will buy through your links if you're into affiliate marketing, traffic that will buy your products if you're an info marketer, and traffic that will hire your services if you're a freelancer.

How soon can you start getting these results?

Well, that depends on certain factors, such as the value of your content, the profitability of your niche, your ability to convince your readers to take action, and the relevance of your offers to your visitors.

But most of the time, with consistency, you can start making money in 6 months. It could be more, and it could be less. But don't start expecting results until after 6 months of consistently completing the tasks listed above.

Bottom line

Most people fail to make money online because they don't take action (even after reading and reading). But even more people fail because they're not consistent.

In essence, consistency is all you need to succeed in online business. This is one of the best secrets you'll ever get to learn about online business. Take my words, and you'll thank me in the near future.

How to Turn Your Blog into a Money Spinner
I always feel like spanking those irritatingly desperate bloggers who start asking questions on how to make money from their blogs after publishing just 8 or 9 posts – mediocre posts at that!

But I don't blame them. I'd rather blame those bloody liars who make them believe that a new blog becomes an ATM machine within 2 weeks.

In reality, blogging (or any other online business) won't make you rich overnight. And the earlier you wake up to this fact, the more immune to frustration you'll become.

To make money from your blog, you need to produce lots of quality content that generates traffic consistently.

When I say traffic, I mean hundreds to thousands of visitors per day. To me, any blog that attracts less than a hundred unique daily visits is still in the making, and such a blog shouldn't be monetized yet.

Only after you've produced quality content enough to make your blog an authority – and after your blog starts attracting hundreds to thousands of visits daily – should you proceed to monetize your blog.

Having discussed various strategies for generating quality traffic to your blog (in previous posts), I'll now discuss how to monetize your blog once you start generating sizeable traffic consistently.

There are many ways to monetize your blog. But I'll be discussing only the 5 most popular and most profitable methods.

1. Selling your own product (or service)

This is the most profitable blog monetization method. You can create your own information product and sell it on your blog. This could be an ebook, a podcast, an e-course series, or other products that your business offers (if you're blogging mainly to promote your offline business).

Similarly, you can advertise your freelance services (if you offer any), such as writing, web design, graphics design, SEO, and so on.

How well your product or service would sell hinges on how well you've been able to establish yourself as an expert. Your readers won't buy your product or service if they're not convinced that you really know your stuff.

This method of monetization affords you maximum control over pricing and handling of transactions. And you'll take all the profit you make.

2. Affiliate marketing

This simply involves selling other people's products and getting a commission from each sale. This option could be very profitable, too – depending on the product you're marketing and how many sales you're making.

As an affiliate marketer, you don't get all the profit from each sale (you only get a commission), and you have no control over the pricing. Nonetheless, there's no limit to how much you can make as an affiliate marketer – the more you sell, the more profit you'll make. And you don't have to deal with the intricacies of handling transaction and delivery issues.

To monetize your blog through affiliate marketing, you need to register with an affiliate network (such as <u>Amazon</u> or <u>Markethealth</u>) or a company that runs an affiliate program. Then you market their products by displaying them in ads on your blog or by adding links to those products within your blog posts.

Bear in mind that you'll only make money via this method if you recommend products that are closely related to your blog's topic. Marketing diamond necklaces on a technology blog is just silly.

3. Displaying contextual ads (Adsense, etc.)

This is the commonest method of blog monetization, as far as I know. It simply involves registering with an ad network and having their ads displayed on your blog. You'll get paid for each click (payper-click model) or for every 1000 views or impressions (pay-permille).

Examples of ad networks include <u>Google Adsense</u> (the most popular), <u>Media.net</u>, <u>Addynamo</u>, <u>Infolinks</u>, <u>Chitika</u>, and so on.

Ads by ad networks are displayed automatically and they're closely related to your content. This is why they tend to attract readers' attention.

4. Displaying private ads

You can sell ad space on your blog to individuals and organizations offering products or services that your readers are likely to be interested in. Here, you're in charge of pricing, and you put up the ads yourself. You also take all the profit.

To attract advertisers, your blog must be generating thousands of daily visits.

5. Publishing paid reviews

This is a more subtle form of advertising. It involves recommending a product or service to your readers through a dedicated blog post – and you charge a fee for doing just that.

One gladdening fact is that you can monetize your blog with more than one of these options. (In fact, I know may blogs that are monetized with all these options.) And this is telling proof that having a blog can fetch you money through many avenues.

Bottom line

A single blog can help you make money through information marketing, freelancing, ad displays, sponsored reviews, and affiliate marketing. This is why I opine that blogging is the mother of all online businesses, and that any serious individual going into online business should focus on starting a blog first.

CHAPTER TEN

5 WAYS YOU CAN RECEIVE PAYMENT ONLINE (ASIDE PAYPAL)

No doubt, PayPal is about the most widely used payment method for online transactions – worldwide. But sadly, Nigerians are no longer allowed to use the service.

This restriction is one of the major worries of Nigerian webmasters and online entrepreneurs. In fact, it is the reason why some Nigerians are yet to start their online businesses.

If you're finding it hard to receive payment online because Paypal is a no-no for we Nigerians, this lesson is for you. Here, I'll be discussing five alternatives to Paypal.

Note that these alternatives may not be perfect replacements for PayPal, but they'll provide an avenue for you to receive payment online. (Of course, half a loaf is better than no bread.)

Now, let's look at the alternatives you've got.

1. Western Union Money Transfer

With this method, you can receive payment from anywhere in the world. If you're a freelancer, this may be a good option for you – provided you have clients that are understanding.

Note that you must have a valid government-issued ID card (such as an international passport, national identity card, or drivers' license) before you can receive payments.

Although this payment method is very speedy, it may not suitable for very small payments due to the transfer and transaction charges.

2. Cheque

If you're planning to venture (or you're already) into affiliate marketing or Google Adsense, receiving a check may be the best (or even the only) option for you. This option is suitable for freelancers, too.

Once you request your payment (from the company or individual you're dealing with), a US cheque (check) would be sent to your mailing address, and you can get your cash at any Nigerian bank.

Receiving funds through cheques may take weeks, depending on the bank you use as well as the issuing bank. So, this payment method may not be suitable if you need the funds urgently.

To receive funds via cheques, you must have a domiciliary account, an international banking account that can be used for sending and receiving payments worldwide. You can easily open a domiciliary account with any Nigerian bank, but you must have a valid identity document (international passport, drivers' license, or national ID card) and other requirements (which vary depending on the bank). You can visit any bank to make enquiries on opening a domiciliary account.

Please note that transaction charges apply to cheques, and these may vary from bank to bank.

WARNING: Have your cheque sent only to a valid mailing address! If your address cannot be traced

easily, you may lose your cheque.

3. Bank Wire transfer

This method of payment is very simple: your funds are transferred from the sender's bank account to your own bank account here in Nigeria. Once again, you'll need a domiciliary account for you to receive payment through this method.

Though speedy as it may seem, this payment method is not instant. You may have to wait for days to a few weeks before receiving your funds. But the option is suitable for almost everyone in online business.

4. Payoneer Mastercard

This is the coolest option for Nigerians (in my opinion). With the Payoneer debit MasterCard, you can receive payment from freelance job sites, affiliate networks, individuals, and companies.

To get your Payoneer debit card, you have two options:

If you're going into online freelance business (writing, web design, programming, SEO, graphics design, virtual assistance, translation, etc.) or affiliate marketing, you can request the card through the freelance outsourcing site or affiliate network you want to work with. Elance, Odesk, Freelancer, Markethealth, and Fiverr are examples of Payoneer partners through which you can request your own card.

Request the card directly through Payoneer's official website.

After your request has been confirmed by the Payoneer

support, you'll be sent an email informing you of the shipment as well as the expected delivery date. (You'd be told to wait for 28 days, but I receive my own cards in less than 20 days. So, it depends on your location in Nigeria.)

WARNING: Payoneer does not deliver to mailboxes. Only residential addresses are allowed. So, use a valid residential address that can be traced easily. If your card gets lost in transit, you may be asked to pay $50 (about N7500) before another card is sent to you.

The Payoneer card allows you to receive direct payment from freelance sites and affiliate networks. Also, individuals can load funds directly to your card from another credit/debit card.

Once you have the funds on your card, you'll get an email notification from Payoneer, and you can withdraw your funds instantly from any ATM that processes Mastercard-issued cards (I only know of GTB and Zenith bank ATMs at the moment).

5. 2Checkout

Also known as 2CO, this service allows you to integrate a payment system on your website or blog. So, if you sell products or render services online, this option is for you.

Just visit 2checkout.com and register. (Note that you'll be charged an application fee of $10.) It takes a few days to get your account approved (they need to confirm that your business is genuine). Once your account is approved, you can set up the payment button on your page.

With 2CO, you can receive payment from anyone, regardless of the payment method that person prefers

(PayPal, credit/debit card, etc.). Subsequently, you can withdraw your funds from your 2CO account. Payment is made every Thursday (provided you have up to the minimum release balance) to your Payoneer Mastercard, or your bank (domiciliary) account via check or Wire transfer.

You can find out more information about 2checkout on their FAQ page (https://www.2checkout.com/faq/).

So, if you've always thought that online business is impossible without PayPal, I'm sure you now know that there are other options for you. Choose your preferred option and start making cool cash from your online business.

Conclusion

Anyone can make money online. It's just about knowing how to go about it the smart way.

Now that you've learned a lot from this ebook, take action. That's how to make all you've learned work for you.

Bear in mind that this book doesn't contain everything that you need to know about online business. So, you'll need to keep learning. And never stop.

Since there's still much to learn, I advise you to check out my blog (http://webincomeplus.com) on a frequent basis. You'll always learn something new by frequently checking out the blog, as I try to publish detailed, valuable, unique, and highly resourceful articles every week.

I wish you success in your attempts to make money online

ABOUT THE AUTHOR

Christopher Abraham Christopher Abraham is an expert in the field of online money making. He has built quite a lot from the internet business and also dedicated in ensuring that others also make it

www.ingramcontent.com/pod-product-compliance
Lightning Source LLC
Chambersburg PA
CBHW070548160726
48003CB00005B/1945